IN MY HEAD

GOWRI ARUN MENON

To those who felt butterflies for their Romeos,
and those who tilted to Juliet more.
To those who like prince charming,
and to those who like the artist more.
To those who find love in simplicity,
and to those who find wonder in extravagance.
To those who get up and daydream,
and to those who are the reasons for the daydreams
To all those who imagine and write,
and to all those who imagine and read
This is for you.

Contents

Foreword

Poetry has the power to express complex emotions and ideas in just a few words, and this collection of poems by Gowri Arun is a testament to that power. In this book, you will find poems that explore love, loss, and the human experience, as well as celebrate the beauty of the natural world.

Gowri's writing is rich with vivid imagery and language that is both powerful and evocative. Through her words, we are transported to different times and places, and invited to see the world through her eyes. Her writing reminds us of the power of poetry to connect us to our own emotions and to the experiences of others.

As you read through this collection, you will find poems that speak to your heart and soul, that make you pause and reflect, and that leave you with a sense of wonder and awe. Whether you are a seasoned poetry reader or new to the genre, this collection is sure to delight and inspire.

I am honored to have had the opportunity to read and appreciate Gowri's work, and I am thrilled to introduce it to a wider audience. I hope that these poems will resonate with you and remind you of the beauty and complexity of the world around us.

Dr.Arun Korath

Preface

I am a daughter, friend and hopeless romantic
so my poems are filled with reflections on
myself, assumptions, and daydreams

Acknowledgements

I would like to express my sincerest gratitude to all those who have supported me in the creation of this poem. First and foremost, I would like to thank my family for their unwavering love and encouragement throughout my writing journey. Their support has been invaluable and has given me the strength to pursue my passion.
I would also like to extend my thanks to my friends, who have offered their feedback and constructive criticism. Their insight has helped me to refine my work and improve my craft.
Furthermore, I am grateful to my teachers and mentors, whose guidance and expertise have been instrumental in shaping my writing. Their mentorship has inspired me to push myself beyond my limits and to strive for excellence in all that I do.
Finally, I would like to thank the readers of my poem, whose appreciation and admiration have motivated me to continue writing. Your support means the world to me, and I am honored to have the opportunity to share my work with you.

1. THE NIGHT AND YOU

As blue and black coat the sky,
when birds no longer fly.
The stars dance tonight,
the moon shining bright,comets getting drunk falling
like light,
the planets standing strong, like knights.
When all noise seems to die,
When children no longer cry,
I look at you,
singing along with the solar crew.
People like you are quite a few,
who don't let the night coat them blue.
You're so beautiful, I seem to love you too.
You should see the way my heart swells.
When I look at you my eyes can't help but dwell.
The night's dark can't hide my love,
my love that reaches the stars and above.
It seems although I can't seem to hold it in now,
when I look at your eyes
all doubt dies.
Or maybe it's just the alcohol he shared with the
comets,
that makes me think I'll have no regrets,
when I tell you I love you.

2. OCTOBER

Some day in October
I wish I could look over
just sit down and wonder
what I have done so far
To call for my lover
to sit with them and wonder
while driving in the car
Thinking of how we met
waiting slowly for time to let
go of everything
but when I see them smiling
I can't help but want to stay
They're so beautiful like the sun's ray
I don't think I'll make it to November
without having to remember
to just sit with you and wonder
I don't know if that's possible however
I would think of last September
when my heart was on fire
like an ember
burning with desire
burning for you till December
I would still sit and wonder
what kind of spell did you put me under
And what could've been
adding on to my sin
to try and forget you
throughout October

3. AS MUCH AS I....

As beautiful as words,
And just as sad
As charming as a prince
With a curse that's cast
As high as a bird
In the eyes of a hunter
As much in love
As much as a star-crossed lover
As wishful as a star
Slowly falling down
As wild as a beast
Without its crown
As much as I love you....

4. HAPPY FIFTEENTH BIRTHDAY

(Oct 24, 2022, for my crush's fifteenth birthday)
You're fifteen now! Yay!
one day I shall catch up with you I pray.
And hopefully, you'll stay.
Maybe when you are fifty,
And you live by the city,
I'll meet you close by!
and maybe you'll remember me.
We'll catch a drink by the sea,
someday when you're thirty.
I hope that through this whole year
your days will be clear!
And may all bad things disappear!
Maybe I'll stick around till sixteen!
You might meet me in between.
Maybe I try and catch your heart.
Maybe we'll float apart.
But I wish you an amazing year!
I wish you dreams,
and hope you achieve all extremes.
I wish you wonder,
may your life be as bright as thunder.
I wish you love
and everything above.
May your year be bright,
and I hope you celebrate tonight

5. MY LOVE

So I met you today!
honey dripping from every word you say.
But I love the way
my cheeks light up like ruby!
just planned my whole life with you, only to be
just another friend, oh dear me.
Oh, but that's quite alright!
Seeing you late at night,
the moon so bright and white,
as you take in all its light
and shine like the stars tonight.
Makes me want to take flight!
Maybe you could be my darling knight,
just for my delight!
My heart jumps and reaches the sky,
when you simply meet my eye!
Every time you come by,
my darling you take me high.
You're just one hell of a guy
who makes me wanna run and cry.
But I simply can't deny,
no matter how shy,
I don't want you to say goodbye

6. A WORLD THROUGH EVER CHANGING EYES

As a student
My world seemed bent
As a child
Everything seems too mild.
As an eighteen-year-old
Life was more beautiful than gold
At thirty
Life seems too boring to me
While the rope around my neck suffocates
And the lies I said no longer feel real
I will apologize to my mom
And the boy I took to prom
My friends I lied to
When I said I had something to do
I'm sorry to my fiancé
(the same boy I took to prom that day)
I'm sorry to my dad
For not asking whether his day was bad
I'm sorry if I make anyone sad
But please don't cry
When I leave I will fly
The rope around my neck will be flowers
Around like a chain, and I will sing by rivers
When you think of me
I want you to be happy
Not how I left but how I stayed
And how beautifully I laid
In the coffin that day

7. A DEAD MAN'S KISS

My heart longs for your love
While my body aches for your touch
When I vowed my life to you
When I smiled and said, "I do…"
I didn't think that you would leave
I wanted to believe
And now that you lie here lifeless
And I stand in a black dress
I'm starting to forget my sanity
It seems like my reality
Just doesn't seem fit
Without you in it
Not one bit
Don't worry for I will be there soon
I will lie with you
My dear

8. YOU WEREN'T IN LOVE.

Sweet words and gentle white lies,
I can forgive everything you haven't apologized for,
when I look into your eyes.
I love you down to the core.
Even if you keep me silent,
when the moon is at its crescent,
I forgive you,
and all that you do.
When you use me at night.
convincing me your some kind of light,
that I need to survive.
That I need to feel alive!
When you run behind that woman,
while telling me you're the only man,
I truly wish you are happy.
Because you won't let me be.
Nor will you let me see.
Each of your smiles
has its lines and lies.
Have you ever been honest?
You make me seem out of my mind!
I still try to remain kind.
I still love you...

9. A FABRICATED LIE

When I cry or when I fly
I want you to be with me
Whether its tomorrow or today
I want to see you stay
When you're at your worst and best
I want to be a shoulder for you to rest
Because even if a tear falls from you
My whole world turns blue
You are someone I'll always remember
Even if my world is burning down like an ember
I want you to look at me
Because I imagine all the things we could be
And I cry thinking about it
That fact I love you to the very last bit
I love you whole
And you play a very important role
In my heart
We could never be apart
But that role is not true
If it's a fabricated lie then what do I do
If I'm not with you
Then how can I fly
I would just cry
While thing about
All the things we could've done
Could've been
And miss you by my side

10. MIRROR

When moons crumble
And stars collapse
When sun dies
And galaxies fall
When forests burn
And seas rise like mountains
When people leave
And your heart aches
I will love you
Love you so much my heart aches
Love you so much I can't leave
My love for you that can move mountains
My love for you burns
And to you who made me fall
My love will never die
When the universe collapses
And all sanity crumbles
Remember I love you

11. HOME

Something always feels amiss when
I'm far from home
A part of me always feels alone
and you can feel it in your bone
Then where is home?
Maybe home is within four walls
Where I used to play with dolls
Where I sleep when night falls
home is my bed
Where I go to rest my head
Home is my mother's arms
home is my lover's silly charms
For some, home is a dead man's heart
Home, for some, Is far apart
home might be unreachable miles away
But in your heart, it will stay
Maybe home is comfort simply
anywhere your heart is happy
Sometimes it's a person you know
or a place you go
somewhere you don't feel low
That is your home

12. TO MY FATHER

He's taller than me!
So much stronger than me!
He could carry me over mountains
and swim through the seas!
He is so much smarter than me!
really nice to me!
He tells me stories of what he sees!
He loves me like no other
and my sweet little brother!
We're a family with my mother!
But my favourite is my father!
He cares for me deep
even in his sleep!
He scares all the monsters away!
He works hard every day!
My father hugs me tight
because he knows thunders a fright!
His eyes shine like diamonds in the night sky!
My mother's too when he looks in her eyes!
They love me, low and high!
My father gives me wings, with him I can fly!
My father is my loving knight!

www.ingramcontent.com/pod-product-compliance
Lightning Source LLC
Chambersburg PA
CBHW040905110726
48005CB00001B/209